KU-274-250

DISASTER PLANNING
FOR LIBRARY AND
INFORMATION SERVICES

John Ashman

The Aslib Know How Series
Editor : Sylvia P Webb

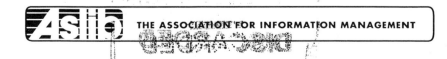

THE ASSOCIATION FOR INFORMATION MANAGEMENT

Published in 1995 by
Aslib, The Association for Information Management
Information House
20-24 Old Street
London
EC1V 9AP

LEEDS METROPOLITAN
UNIVERSITY LIBRARY
1701294395
B14S
309086   12.10.95
025.8   ASH
18 OCT 1995 £9.50

© John Ashman, 1995

Except as otherwise permitted under the Copyright, Designs and Patents Act
1988, this publication may only be reproduced, stored or transmitted in any
form or by any means, with the prior permission in writing of the publisher,
or in the case of reprographic reproduction, in accordance with the terms of a
licence issued by the Copyright Licensing Agency. Enquiries concerning
reproduction outside those terms should be sent to Aslib, The Association for
Information Management, at the above address.

John Ashman asserts his moral rights to be identified as the author of this work
in accordance with sections 77 and 78 of the Copyright, Designs and Patents
Act 1988.

***

British Library Cataloguing in Publication Data
A catalogue record for this book is available from the British Library
ISBN 0 85142 337 X

Aslib, The Association for Information Management, has some two
thousand corporate members worldwide. It actively promotes better
management of information resources.

Aslib lobbies on all aspects of the management of and legislation
concerning information. It provides consultancy and information
services, professional development training, specialist recruitment, and
publishes primary and secondary journals, conference proceedings,
directories and monographs.

Further information about Aslib can be obtained from :
Aslib, The Association for Information Management
Information House, 20-24 Old Street, London, EC1V 9AP
Tel: +(44) 71 253 4488, Fax: +(44) 71 430 0514
Email: aslib@aslib.demon.co.uk

Series Editor - Sylvia P. Webb

Sylvia Webb is a well known consultant, author and lecturer in the information management field. Her first book 'Creating an Information Service' was published by Aslib and has sold in over forty countries. She has experience of working in both the public and private sectors, ranging from public libraries to national and international organisations. She has also been a lecturer at Ashridge Management College, specialising in management and inter-personal skills, which led to her second book, 'Personal Development in Information Work', also published by Aslib. She has served on a number of government advisory bodies and is Chair of the Information and Library Services Lead Body which develops National Vocational Qualifications (NVQs) for the LIS profession. She is actively involved in professional education with Aslib and the Library Association and is also a former Vice-President of the Institute of Information Scientists. As well as being editor of this series, Sylvia Webb has also written two of the Know How Guides: 'Making a charge for library and information services' and 'Preparing a guide to your library and information service'.

A list of titles in the Aslib Know How Series
appears on the back cover of this volume.

Dedication

To Angela, Emily and Lewis.

Thanks are due to Henry Heaney, University Librarian and Keeper of the Hunterian Books and Manuscripts, for permission to use material originally developed at Glasgow University as part of the Library's guidelines for disaster response.

Contents

1. Introduction

In the last thirty years disaster planning has come to be seen as a central management concern in many libraries. The floods in Florence in 1966 became headline news around the world and led to an unprecedented effort to salvage property and holdings involving experts from several countries. The planning need started to become clear to the library world as the scale of the damage and its long-term consequences became apparent. This message has been reinforced each time a disaster has struck a major library or records centre:

- the fire at the Klein Law Library, Temple University, Philadelphia, in 1972, requiring the rapid removal of about 160,000 books following which tens of thousands of volumes were sent for freezing and were dried in a vacuum chamber;

- the fire at the Military Personnel Records Center, Overland, Missouri, in 1973, in which 10,000 cu ft of records were damaged, leading to the need to organize the rapid rescue of large quantities of material before one of the floors was demolished for safety reasons;

- the flood at the Meyer Library, Stanford University, California, in 1978; due to a burst in an eight inch water main leading to damage to nearly 52,000 volumes.

- the fire at the Los Angeles Public Library, California, in April 1986, in which 400,000 volumes were lost and a further 1,700,000 were damaged.

- the fire at the Library of the Academy of Sciences of the Soviet Union, Leningrad, in February 1988, in which 400,000 volumes were destroyed by fire and a further 11,000,000 volumes were damaged by water and smoke.

The financial cost of salvaging and replacing material damaged in such incidents has been found to be very high indeed, but the cost to the institutions in terms of interruption to business, and the cost to its users in wasted time and lost opportunities would be hard for anyone to calculate. Two basic needs emerge from these experiences: firstly a need to reduce the likelihood of further disasters by recognising the threats and taking the necessary preventative action; and secondly a need to ensure that the library is adequately prepared to deal with any further emergency causing damage to the holdings, and will be better placed in future to deal with the situation efficiently and effectively.

Though all the examples cited above involve damage to traditional library materials and paper records caused by fire or flood, consideration also needs to be given to other factors, including our increasing reliance on technology. Senior management should decide how disaster planning needs to be handled within the management structure of the organization as a whole, and consider setting up an Emergency Planning Group, including:

- the head of administration with responsibility for staff and buildings;

- someone with broad collection management responsibility;

- someone with overall responsibility for computer systems;

- and an external adviser with experience of disaster planning (or someone with expertise in conservation who might act in an advisory capacity).

While much of the detailed work involved in drawing up the plans may need to be delegated (e.g. technical questions to do with computer systems), the group should ensure that all aspects of the subject are covered and the needs of users and all staff are taken into account. As with any type of organizational planning, there will be a need to involve people at various levels. A common cause of failure in planning is the lack of commitment to it, or sense of ownership in the plan, felt by those who are required to carry out the tasks that make it work. It may be worthwhile bringing together a number of committed colleagues from several libraries, representing various library systems or other institutions, to form a single Planning Group to assist each member of the consortium or network to develop its own disaster plans appropriate to its particular needs. Cooperating institutions need not be of exactly the same type, or equal in size, provided that they form a natural grouping and that they recognise common interests and share similar problems.

The term *library* as used here includes information services generally, as these guidelines are intended for all professional people working in libraries, archives, record centres and so on. In the event of a disaster, the normal management system of the affected institution becomes the system for handling the crisis (the head of administration probably acting as disaster response co-ordinator). Their task is to maintain or re-establish at least a partial service, and to ensure that staff and users understand the cause of the problem and the efforts being made to restore services to optimal levels. Any member of the consortium or network which suffers significant damage as a result of a fire, flood, etc., should ensure that a report is written (including recommendations for improvements in existing plans, if necessary), and circulated to members of the Planning Group. It may also be desirable for co-operating institutions to help in an emergency by lending staff, equipment or materials to assist another member of the network in the salvage of damaged holdings.

Safety of personnel will be the first concern of the Planning Group. Normally written procedures will already exist concerning the evacuation of the building in the case of fire. Thought may be given to developing written procedures to cover other possible situations such as severe storms, earthquake, civil disorder or bomb threat. Where the library forms part of a larger organization, the practices adopted by the parent body will naturally have an influence. Management should consider at the outset how it intends to use the term 'disaster planning' bearing in mind that the word 'disaster' usually refers to an event that comes upon us suddenly, causing great distress or damage and its use could suggest a negative or pessimistic outlook. The term 'emergency planning' may be more appropriate at times.

In preparing these guidelines, it has been decided to exclude from consideration threats which cannot be adequately quantified such as problem users, book theft, mutilation and mishandling of books, and those causes of damage which are known to act over a long period of time, such as the chemical deterioration of paper due to acidity. These problems have sometimes been referred to in the literature as 'slow disasters' or as the 'quiet disaster'.

This guide begins with a section on disaster prevention, then goes on to discuss the question of how to compile your own emergency planning handbook. Guidelines on dealing with the most common types of disaster involving damage to books, documents, photographic materials, etc., due to fire, flood, etc., have been divided into two parts. The first part deals with the initial action needed to stabilize the condition of water-damaged materials and the second part deals with the need for the conservation of damaged materials at a later date.

Throughout the main text the term 'books' is used as shorthand for monographs, journals, official publications, reports and other documents whether printed or written by hand. The term 'non-book media' used in this guide includes microforms, photographs, audio and video tapes, CDs, computer tapes and discs.

2. Disaster prevention

Aims: To protect the library from disaster by improving its standard operating procedures, and to reduce the risk of damage to the holdings to acceptable levels.

A formal risk assessment may be conducted as a preliminary step towards creating or reviewing disaster planning procedures. This should identify what sort of problems might lead to loss or damage to holdings or breakdown of service, and what the consequences might be for your business. Risk assessment may lead to improved building maintenance and security, and may help determine whether new agreements need to be made with suppliers and service providers which will reduce exposure to risk. The process of assessment may be prompted by the need to ensure that adequate insurance cover is provided.

Identifying matters for immediate action

It may not be possible to make all the necessary changes immediately, but it might be worthwhile to devise a scheme to separate problems into those where remedies can be introduced without too much delay and those which demand a longer-term approach, due perhaps to the need for building alterations. It would also make sense to list all the potential improvements, noting the resources required, and to determine priorities for both short- and long-term planning.

New technology and security copying

Maintain strict routines to ensure computer data is adequately backed up. Several copies may be needed. It is common for several generations of back-ups to be kept. Back-ups need to be stored well away from each other so that all copies cannot be damaged by the same incident. Damaged computer equipment can destroy the information on back-ups, so the procedures governing access to back-ups need to be carefully thought out. There are numerous ways in which computer data can be lost through failure to back it up, and through damage occurring to the back-ups. Other sources of dangers include hacking, interruptions to the power supply, use of poor quality hardware, and computer viruses. Passwords should be kept secret and may need to be changed regularly. Great care should be taken to locate central computer equipment in as safe a place as possible.

Magnetic media (computer tapes, floppy disks, audio and video tapes), should be stored away from strong magnetic fields. Manufacturers warn against leaving these materials next to any electronic equipment. Some security devices could also damage these materials for similar reasons.

Irreplaceable holdings in your care could be photographed, photocopied, microfilmed or digitized for use with a computer to provide back-up copies. The existence of these copies may lessen the seriousness of loss or damage to the originals. If it is planned to make copies to serve in this way, master copies should be made, and these should be stored in a safe place as security copies. Security copies are not used for everyday reference and copying purposes, but kept strictly in reserve under controlled conditions.

The format of information on security or archival copies may need to be updated. Video tapes and computer media are only good as long as there are appropriate machines to read them.

Building maintenance, safety and security

Fire prevention and safety
Consider seeking professional advice on matters of fire prevention and safety. The local Fire Service may have a Fire Prevention Officer who can offer advice free of charge. Where the library comes under a college, or university, a government department or other large organization, those with overall responsibility for fire prevention matters in the institution should also be made aware of the nature of the library's holdings and of any special needs, and may act as liaison with the Fire Service. Arson is a common cause of fire in libraries.

Recommendations:

- In large organizations, periodic safety inspections should be conducted so as to ensure that any faults which have not already been reported or have not been rectified receive attention. Electricians may need to be called in to check specific wiring faults, in addition to any regular checks that may be made on the wiring system in general. Ageing or damaged wiring is a common cause of fire.

- All buildings should have hand-held fire extinguishers in addition to hosereels or sprinklers. Staff need to be aware of the different types of extinguisher available and the types of fire for which they are suitable. Training may be available in the use of extinguishers. It is recommended that all fire-fighting equipment be regularly checked to ensure that it is still where it should be and is in working order. Where a particular member of staff has been given responsibility for seeing that checks are done, this person is usually designated the Fire Officer. The Fire Officer would normally also have responsibility for liaison with the building maintenance department (where one exists), and other fire prevention experts.

- All buildings should have adequate means of raising the alarm. Manually operated alarms of the "break glass to sound alarm" type and smoke or heat detectors are recommended. Where automatic fire alarms exist, regular testing of the system is recommended. Fire drills will also need to be organized. Where automatic systems exist there may be a number of false alarms. Practice drills should be organized to ensure that procedures are tested regularly. Evacuation may be timed, and arrangements could be made so that the Fire Officer can tell if there are bottle necks in certain exits and whether all available exits are being used.

- Smoking should only be permitted in designated areas due to the risk of fire. However, all staff have a responsibility for ensuring that fire regulations are complied with in the areas in which they work: e.g. certain doors are kept locked, other doors are kept unlocked, and fire exits are kept free of obstruction, flammable liquids are stored in safety cupboards where necessary, flammable packing materials are kept tidy, and rubbish is put in the proper place.

Security routines
Consider seeking professional advice on security matters. The police may have a Crime Prevention Officer who can offer advice free of charge. Make certain that all new members of staff are made aware of the need for good building security, are trained in routines to ensure that windows and doors are closed and locked as necessary. Reminders may need to be issued from time to time to ensure that staff secure doors and windows in the areas in which they work. Unless there is a janitor or other person with general responsibility for security available, it is important that a trusted member of staff be nominated to check doors and windows in all other areas, such as cloakroom and toilets.

Recommendations:

- All keys left in the building should be kept in a secure, unobtrusive place. If a key case is used, the key to the key case would normally be given to a member of the security or janitorial staff, be taken home by a trusted member of staff, or concealed well away from the key case.

- A proper check should be kept when keys to the building are issued, and an up-to-date list should be kept of every key held by each member of staff. It is important to maintain confidentiality concerning all security systems and devices in use in the library, especially those that protect rare books and display cases. When any maintenance work is being undertaken on the premises out-of-hours, library staff may need to ensure that security surveillance is provided. Where cleaners need access to the building out-of-hours to undertake routine cleaning work, it is generally advised that one trusted person only should have the keys, whether one of the cleaners, a security guard or janitor.

- Any loss of keys should be reported at once. Locks may need to be changed if keys are not found. Insurance cover may be affected if appropriate action is not taken.

Building maintenance and surveillance
Ensure all staff know how to report faulty locks, broken catches or window panes, etc., and that action is taken promptly.

Recommendations:

- Heating and air-conditioning systems should be regularly checked and serviced. Regular inspections could also be organized to check gutters, and drains to ensure they are free from blockage, to check roofs, skylights, and windows for damage or water penetration.

- Where the building has the benefit of an out-of hours security patrol or there is a person on duty on the premises with responsibility for security matters, such staff should be kept informed as to which areas are most vulnerable and a prioritized list should be drawn up so that routine checks can be made.

- Fire exits which cannot be kept locked (because they need to serve as public exits), can be fitted with electronic alarms. If such alarms are powered by battery, batteries should be replaced regularly according to the manufacturer's recommendations. Training should be given so that staff know what to do when members of the public are found using the fire exits and alarms are set off. If there is no member of staff nearby, the alarm may prove useless. Consideration might be given to the installation of a video camera at the exit, or at other points.

- Ground floor and basement level windows can be fitted with toughened glass. Where windows have been broken by vandals or during a break-in, repairs should be undertaken as soon as possible, using toughened glass in preference to ordinary glass.

Storage and relocation of stock

Storing high value materials
Ensure any irreplaceable holdings or materials of high value (including unique copies of shelf lists, indexes, etc.) are stored in those parts of the building with the best security and environmental conditions.

Recommendations:

- Shelving systems should be strong, stable and non-flammable. Metal shelving with a non-flammable paint or coating is preferred. Where sub-standard shelving must be used it may be possible to ensure that all the most important materials are kept on the better shelving.

- Stock should not be left in direct contact with the floor. It is recommended that the bottom level of storage systems should be at least six inches from the floor, especially in areas where there is danger of flooding. If the bottom shelf cannot be raised, it may be necessary to leave it empty.

Protecting stock in situ and relocation of stock at risk
Ensure serious consideration is given to the possibility of relocating holdings which are threatened by construction work. Any such undertaking should be carefully planned, as relocation of the stock may in itself become a cause of danger due to the opportunities that are presented for damage to occur during the move. Shrink-wrapping has been used as a way of protecting the collections. A number of large projects have been undertaken in which books and bundles of documents have been sealed in plastic film to protect them *in situ* while construction work proceeds or to protect holdings which have to be moved to new buildings.

Recommendations:

- Polythene sheeting can be used to protect shelving while any sort of dusty work is in progress. However, it should be borne in mind that dust often travels much further than is anticipated and is likely to penetrate any gaps in the sheeting. The work involved in cleaning up after the workmen have left the site may be much more than anticipated. If demolition work is taking place, dust may be a special problem, but checks should be made for blocked downpipes and drains, as they can easily become blocked by rubble or debris and flooding (or a long-term damp problem) may result.

- If roof repairs are being carried out, any shelving underneath the working area should at least be protected with polythene sheeting. Work done below ground may result in flooding.

- Adequate liaison should be established with building contractors, or other workmen working in or adjacent to your building, either directly or through the building maintenance department. The staff responsible for the general care, fetching and reshelving of the stock need to obtain as clear a view as possible of any work being carried out and any special hazards which may arise as a consequence of that work, so that proper measures can be taken to prevent damage to the holdings. Adequate notice of what is to happen will be needed if proper precautions are to be taken.

Building design

It may be worth trying to establish which would be the most desirable building features to create the optimum environment for the library's holdings, and then to work towards meeting the requirements identified. If a new building or extension or major refurbishment is proposed, consider employing a consultant with a knowledge of library needs. A 'Crime Prevention Design Adviser' or 'Architectural Liaison Officer' may be employed specially to advise at the concept, planning, and design stages. Consider asking the Police whether they offer an advisory service.

Building standards

Ensure that all new buildings for library use, and refurbishment of existing accommodation, conforms to the highest standards of safety and fire resistance with regard to both building structures and materials. The design of the library building should be appropriate to the geography of the area in which it is sited and the local climate. There may be a risk of flooding from nearby rivers, or danger of tropical storms, and in some parts of the world buildings need to be resistant to earthquakes. Where hot or cold conditions are a problem, good insulation and ventilation will be particularly important. In a damp climate a pitched roof might be high on your list of desirable building features. Expert advice may be available from national building research organizations.

Recommendations:

- No water or drainage pipes should cross storage areas other than those which form part of an automatic fire extinguishing system. The type of pipework used in such a system may need to be carefully evaluated in terms of its susceptibility to corrosion and failure at the joints.

- An adequate number of stopcocks should be fitted to the water supply system to allow water to be turned off in the event of a burst or leak, or for any other reason. Where hosereels are provided for fire-fighting purposes it is recommended that isolating valves are fitted so as to prevent leakage from the system.

- In those areas which do carry water supplies, a cavity should be provided extending down to a level lower than the storage areas, so that leaking water can be drained away safely. Sump pumps can be situated in the lowest level of the cavity where there are no drains at that level. Sump pumps can be provided with sensors and be self activating, and alarms can be fitted to indicate that the pumps have been activated.

- Rear doors that are not required as emergency exits or as essential service doors should be eliminated. Essential rear doors can be made to open outwards to assist in evacuation in an emergency. Doors which open inwards are generally easier to kick in. If hinges must be exposed on the outside of the building, they may need to be covered or strengthened. Bars or security grills may also be recommended for doors, windows and skylights concealed from the street.
- Locks on external doors should be renewed periodically. Double-cylinder dead-bolt latches are recommended.

Alarm systems

Ensure that basic building security is adequate for the size and value of the holdings, and consider whether any automatic alarm systems are required. Each building poses its own particular problems and these should be discussed in detail with those responsible for planning and undertaking major changes. A significant number of fires in libraries have been attributed to arson following break-ins.

Recommendations:

- Where adequate cover cannot be maintained by security or janitorial staff out-of-hours, the building should be fitted with an automatic intruder or burglar alarm system linked to a central watch station (possibly miles away from the protected property), where the alarm signal can be received when the library is closed. In some cases alarms need only be fitted to those parts of the building which are vulnerable to break-ins, or which contain the most valuable material.

- Automatic fire alarm systems with smoke detectors are recommended. In a large building, it can take a long time to find the exact location of the fire, so an automatic monitoring system, which indicates which sensors have been triggered, is to be preferred. In addition, automatic fire extinguishing systems can be installed. These are usually water sprinkler systems, but gaseous systems are also available for special purposes. Automatic sprinklers with highly localized controls are recommended for libraries. These are designed so that water is directed only at those areas where evidence of fire has been detected. The risk of water damage due to unnecessary activation of the sprinklers must be weighed against the risk of letting the fire get out of control.

- Where automatic fire detection or suppression systems are installed, they can be wired to electromagnetic door locks which open only when the alarm is triggered, or when someone at a central point in the library cuts the power.

- Flow-meter alarms can be fitted to the mains supply to indicate when the water is escaping from the system and other alarms can be fitted to water tanks.

3. Disaster preparedness

Aims: To identify the key personnel and resources likely to be involved in dealing with an emergency, and to provide the information and training necessary to ensure an effective response.

For most libraries disaster planning means finding a model or outline plan which can be adapted to its own needs, or joining a consortium or network of libraries which has already developed its own outline plans. Fortunately many national libraries and other institutions with important historical collections have assumed a leadership role, providing advice on various aspects of disaster planning, and serving as sources of information regarding local suppliers and other professional services. Time and effort spent in identifying which materials are irreplaceable, or would be difficult to replace, could be well worthwhile; false assumptions may lead to costly mistakes being made. In the event of a disaster, the resources available to salvage the holdings may need to be concentrated in 'priority areas'. The difficulty of identifying such materials will vary depending on the type of material and the circumstances in different institutions.

Compiling a handbook

An Emergency Planning Handbook must be readable, well researched, organized and concise, and be relevant to local needs. Salvage procedures should be clearly explained. A step-by-step guide could be made available for wide circulation.

Information will also be needed on products and services, but this would best be presented as a separate section, and would need to be kept up-to-date. An up-to-date staff list may also be required, giving the current contact details of all staff likely to be needed in organizing a disaster response team. However, full information need not be circulated to everyone.

Consider whether there would be a need to prepare two editions of the handbook, one for general circulation and one for limited distribution. Decide who will be responsible for the initial production and revision of an emergency planning handbook. The handbook need not and should not contain all possible information relating to the management of emergencies, but should cover all essential information and may indicate where further information can be found.

11

Floor plans and salvage procedures

Ensure information for use in an emergency is presented as clearly as possible. Salvage procedures may need to be summarized, but try to avoid oversimplifying things.

Suggestions:

- Provide floor plans to identify where fire extinguishers are kept, and the location of points where electricity, water, and gas can be turned off in an emergency, and to give other useful information.

- Include diagrams to illustrate options or to indicate the expected sequence of events. See figures 1 and 2.

- Include a sample form on which damaged library materials can be listed and described. These forms can be used to show what has been damaged, where to locate it and how much damage it has suffered. See figure 3.

- Provide guidelines in the form of information sheets that can be copied and used as handouts when briefing a salvage team. Topics might include packing damaged materials for dispatch, and air drying and interleaving water-damaged materials (see chapter 4).

Evacuation procedures and precautionary measures

Provide a summary of emergency evacuation procedures. Points covered may include assisting the disabled, the need to remain calm and to refrain from spreading rumours, the use of assembly areas and the need to avoid blocking streets or evacuation routes. Consider including guidelines on how to deal with the following:

- *Power failure.* Staff may be asked to check any battery-operated equipment and back-up power sources as soon as the possibility of power failure or a severe storm warning is received. Information may be offered regarding emergency lighting, and what to do if trapped in a lift or elevator.

- *Severe storms.* Procedures may cover how to respond to warnings of severe weather such as winter storms, thunderstorms, tornados, and hurricanes. Staff may be advised to board up windows, to open windows slightly on the side away from the direction in which the storm is coming, to tie down loose items located outside or to bring them indoors.

- *Flooding.* May include the need to beware of electrical hazards, to move valuables and emergency supplies to upper floors, and to store drinking water safely.

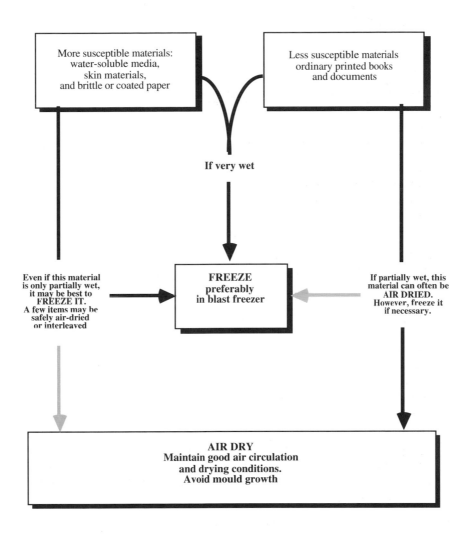

Figure 1 - Salvaging books and documents

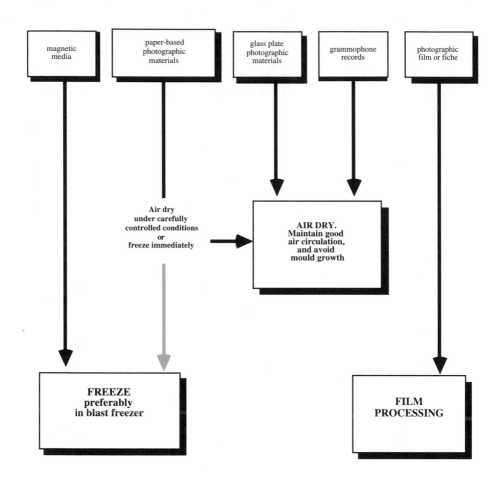

Figure 2 - Salvaging non-book media

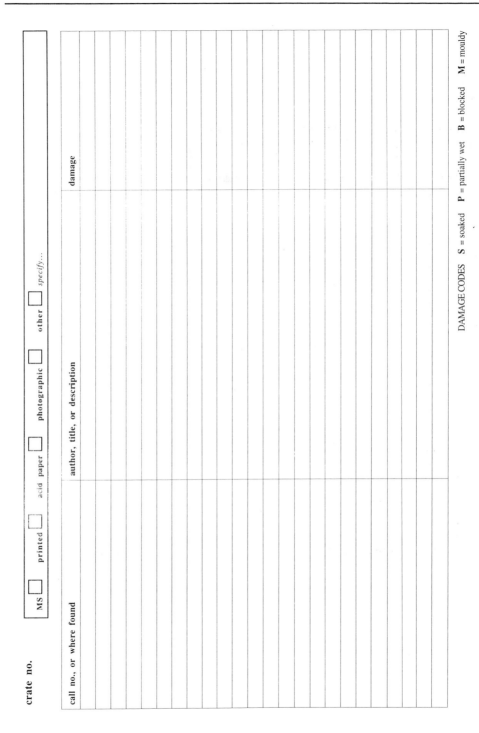

Figure 3 - Damage list form

- *Earthquake*. Should include advice on precautions to take during the shaking, and the sort of hazards to watch for after shaking has stopped.

- *Bombs*. Instructions could be provided on how to deal with a bomb threat received over the telephone. The police may be able provide recommendations or a checklist. Instructions could also be provided on how to recognize and deal with bombs concealed in letters and packages. The postal service may be able to provide a checklist.

- *Explosion and civil disorder*. Instructions may be given to ensure staff refrain from loitering and sightseeing, and on the need to take cover in the event of a gas explosion or bomb warning and to beware of further explosions and special hazards.

Priorities

High value holdings
Ensure that information is available on the location of the most important or valuable materials in each building or part of the building, which may be useful in the event of an emergency in which the holdings are damaged or are placed at risk. It may be necessary to restrict access to such information for security reasons.

Recommendations:

- Information should be easy to follow in an emergency so that priority material can be located quickly. The use of floor plans, or marks on the shelves, might be easier to use than lists. Some form of colour coding might be used but should not be relied on entirely as lighting in an emergency may be poor.

- Holdings which are of high value and are irreplaceable, or would be hard to replace, should be identified as closely as possible. This may include rare book and manuscript collections, maps and photographic collections, any irreplaceable catalogues, lists, or administrative records. Electronic back-up records should also be noted if they are kept on the same site as their counterparts

- Copies of documents identifying priority materials should be made available to Fire Officers and staff responsible for organizing the salvage of damaged materials, but may need to be returned after use for security reasons, depending on the type of information included.

Computer systems
Ensure that adequate technical information is available on the computer systems, and that the priorities for recovery are set out clearly. In the event of

a disaster affecting computing services, staff should be told what damage has been sustained and what problems to expect. Staff should be trained in manual procedures and be prepared to explain to users what has happened. See chapter 6 for further reading on planning for disaster recovery of computer data.

Key personnel

Provide a list of key personnel likely to be involved in responding to a disaster (either by name or by job title). Some libraries make a call-out list with home addresses and telephone numbers so that key personnel can be contacted out-of-hours. It is often suggested that if a disaster occurs it is more likely to be outside normal working hours. The following terms are used in this guide and might serve as headings:

- *Head of Administration, Fire Officer, Duty Officers.* Who will be called out to deal with an emergency in the first instance? Is there a different procedure for out-of-hours emergencies? How will contact be made with the building maintenance department, or with tradesmen, such as electricians and plumbers? In larger facilities, it may be necessary to maintain a rota so that there is always a designated duty officer available to respond to emergencies and to oversee the evacuation of the building. In the case of an out-of-hours emergency, the duty officer may report to the head of administration at the beginning of the following day.

- *Emergency Planning Group, Emergency Planning Handbook, Emergency Planning Network (or Consortium).* It is suggested that a planning group be set up including the head of administration with responsibility for staff and buildings, someone with broad collection management responsibility, someone with overall responsibility for computer systems, and an external adviser with experience of disaster planning (or someone with expertise in conservation) who might act in an advisory capacity. Several libraries, library systems (or other institutions), might be joined together in a network. The planning group would probably have overall control over the production of the emergency planning manual.

- *Disaster Response Co-ordinator, Disaster Response Team, Group Organizers.* Who would normally co-ordinate disaster response? How will a response team be organized? Which members of staff or what categories of staff are likely to be needed? A response team may include subject specialists or other members of staff with special knowledge of the holdings who can help to identify priority materials, conservation staff or external advisers who are prepared to assist. The team may need to be organized into a number of distinct groups allocated to different tasks or working in different parts of the building or in different buildings.

17

Directory of products and services

List facilities offering services and include local suppliers if possible. Consider arranging entries under the following headings:

- *Blast Freezing and Cold Storage.* Include as many local facilities as possible as a single facility may not have sufficient capacity for your needs given your likely requirement for immediate and rapid action. Be prepared to telephone around to find out what space is available when necessary. Local frozen food retailers may be willing to offer some freezer space, and university laboratories may have suitable facilities, but do not include these types of facility on a list intended for general circulation without first obtaining the permission of those in charge. If books are wet and mouldy or are contaminated by sewage or chemicals, it may not be possible to use normal freezer space.

- *Equipment Hire and Transport Services.* List the type of equipment available. Items of particular interest might include crates, dehumidifiers, fans, pumps, electricity generators and emergency lighting. Freezer trucks may be needed to take wet books to the blast freezer and on to a cold store or to freeze or vacuum drying facilities. Freezer trucks are generally only needed if the journey will take two hours or more.

- *Freeze or Vacuum Drying Facilities.* Identify the type of process available. Note the capacity of the equipment and the organisation's previous experience in disaster recovery.

- *Film Processors.* Some facilities may be able to treat flood-damaged microfilm etc., and may have previous experience.

- *Disaster Recovery.* Companies may specialize in disaster recovery or 'business continuation', the back up and recovery of computer data, the salvage of library books and documents, the salvage of photographic materials, or offer a service which includes all of those things. Establish which services the organization itself undertakes and which it will sub-contract.

Maintaining up-to-date contact information
Include addresses, telephone, and fax numbers, and give the names or positions of personnel most likely to be able to help. List particular services or products offered where necessary. It may be possible to get information from other libraries who have already made similar enquiries and made contact with the people providing the services you may need. Information must to be reliable and up-to-date.

Points to consider:

- The Directory may be compiled and updated on computer, but ensure that there is also a printed copy available in case access to computer data is not possible.

- If a commercially produced directory is available, consider providing a copy with the staff handbook or indicate where the directory can be found.

Equipment and materials for use in emergencies

It is recommended that some equipment and materials should be purchased or set aside for use in emergencies only. Supplies should not be borrowed or used for any other purpose, and may need to be locked up. Notices could be posted to warn against misuse. Quantities kept may depend on the size of the library and the perceived risk to the holdings.

If there is a danger of coming into contact with sewage water or water contaminated by chemicals, special safety equipment may be needed. This might include one-piece protective clothing which covers the body head to foot, a face shield and breathing apparatus. In these circumstances the library should call for expert assistance so as to prevent its staff being exposed to unwarranted danger and to ensure that the situation is dealt with as effectively as possible.

Acquire all or a selection of the following:

- *Torches or flashlights.* To ensure that this type of equipment is always available for immediate use, it is suggested that leakproof batteries only should be left in lamps and all batteries replaced at regular intervals according to the manufacturer's recommendations.

- *Clear polythene sheeting.* Rolls of medium or heavy duty polythene can be purchased to cover shelving to keep it clean and dry, or to cover floors, tables and equipment. Sheeting could be secured by the use of string or water-resistant self-adhesive tape.

- *Pumps.* Submersible hand-operated or electric pumps are available. A length of hose will also be needed to attach to the pump in order to take the water outside the building, or to a sump or drain within the building. The pump will reduce the water level quickly and will be most effective when there is an inch or more depth of water. If water still remains after the pump has removed all it can, use a wet vacuum cleaner or mop.

- *Wet vacuum cleaners and mops.* Vacuum cleaners are available with a drum which will take water as well as dirt. Cleaners described as 'wet or dry' may need to be adapted by adding or removing the dust bag before use. If the cleaner is reserved for wet use only, the dust bag should be removed and a notice could be posted indicating that it has been adapted and is not suitable for dry use.

19

- *Buckets.* Buckets can be used for cleaning purposes but can also be used for the salvage of microfilm, etc., in which case close-fitting lids are recommended.

- *Paper for interleaving.* Newsprint has been used to interleave water-damaged books to dry out the leaves and to prevent their sticking together. This type of paper (i.e. unprinted newspaper) is cheap, but it discolours and becomes quite acidic if stored for a long time. It is better to buy a good quality paper to hold in stock, such as Whatman paper Grade 114. (Whatman paper can be obtained in the UK from Whatman Paper Ltd, Specialty Products Division, Springfield Mill, Maidstone, Kent ME14 2LE) The use of coloured paper is not recommended for interleaving as the colour may transfer to the document and cause serious damage.

- *First Aid supplies.* This should include all the standard components such as bandages, dressings, scissors, and safety pins.

Protective clothing

Acquire all or a selection of the following:

- *Waterproof aprons, coats and trousers.* Cheap disposable plastic aprons can be bought in bulk for use in laboratories. Suitable coats and trousers may be found in catalogues of safety equipment (along with safety helmets and gloves). Disposable water-resistant (paper-based) clothing may be suitable, being lighter and cooler to wear than other types.

- *Safety helmets.* A few plastic helmets of the type used in the construction industry could be stocked. They are usually one-size, and adjusted to fit by means of a strap inside the hat.

- *Waterproof boots.* Different sizes will need to be stocked.

- *Gloves.* Cheap white cotton gloves sold as examination gloves may be useful. "Surgical" plastic gloves (often identical gloves for right or left hand) may be needed, especially for handling wet photographic materials. Rubber or plastic gloves may be too hot to wear for long periods, however, or too slippery for some work.

Cleaning and packing supplies

Acquire all or a selection of the following:

- *Cloths and sponges.* A variety of absorbent cleaning cloths, sponges or sponge cloths could be stocked. Cloths are often preferred for heavy use.

- *Disposable paper.* Rolls of absorbent white paper could be stocked, preferably industrial or commercial rolls about 18 inches (or 500 mm) wide.

- *Clear polythene bags.* These bags are best obtained from wholesale suppliers who stock packaging materials for commercial use. They are available in a great variety of sizes and at reasonable prices if bought in quantity. Bags can be used when packing books to be sent off-site for treatment, and for collecting together badly damaged materials for later sorting. Transparent plastic is to be preferred as the contents remain visible.

Record keeping and communications

Acquire all or a selection of the following or consider hiring equipment as needed:

- *Pencils, notepads and labels.* Pencils should not be used to write on wet or damp paper. If you do use them, choose pencils which are not too hard. Pens may cause problems as the ink is liable to run in contact with water and cause serious damage. Tie-on labels are likely to be safer than self-adhesive labels. The use of self-adhesive labels or tape may lead to problems when working with wet documents or in other difficult conditions.

- *Damage list forms.* A small stock of forms may prove useful so as to get started without having to wait for supplies to arrive.

- *Tape recorders or dictating machines.* Filling out forms may prove difficult and time-consuming. It may be better to record information on a dictating machine for transfer on to forms or on to computer at a later date. If they are not already available within the organisation it may be possible to hire machines locally when they are needed from office equipment suppliers.

- *Video camera.* A video camera can be used for the same purpose as a dictating machine, but has the added benefit of recording pictures too. Video pictures may save time spent in making detailed verbal descriptions.

- *Telephones.* If the telephones are not working, communications may be extremely difficult and could considerably hamper progress in dealing with a disaster. Two-way radios or cellular telephones may be available for hire from radio communications equipment specialists.

Staff education

Staff education may need to be organized in cooperation with other libraries, especially in the case of smaller facilities. Exchange of ideas between libraries would in any case be beneficial. A simulated small-scale disaster could be set up. These events generally involve some 'hands-on' experience with wet books, but the main benefit is often in the way it brings people together and develops team spirit. No attempt should be made to teach conservation skills as part of disaster preparedness training.

Training of Duty Officers

Ensure duty officers are trained in how to respond in the event of an emergency involving damage to the holdings. Guidance should be offered regarding procedures to be followed when a crisis occurs outside normal working hours. The responsibilities of duty officers may include the following:

- *The safety of users and staff.* The duty officer will need to take account of any special health and safety factors relating to the particular cause of damage, as well as normal procedures for evacuation.

- *The security of the building.* Tradesmen such as locksmiths, glaziers, joiners, and electricians, may need to be called out.

- *Prevention of further damage to the holdings.* Initial action might include gaining entry to the disaster area, rough assessment of damage, deciding what can be done with existing resources, requesting that water, heating, or electricity be cut off (if not already required on safety grounds), calling for the assistance of other staff, protection of undamaged stock *in situ*, and proceeding with the salvage of damaged materials, bearing in mind the urgency of the situation. Reference may be made to existing guidelines indicating how long water-damaged photographic materials can be left before irreversible damage will occur, and noting the need to take account of the speed with which mould can develop on damp library materials.

Annual seminar or briefing

Organize an annual disaster-preparedness seminar or briefing. In larger institutions with a significant turn-over of staff, a seminar could be organized in-house as an annual event, but ideally this should be integrated into an existing programme of staff education where one already exists. Such a programme may be aimed mainly at trainee staff (and is distinct from induction training), but attendance should be open to all.

Recommendations:

- Presentations should be given by a member of the planning group, or by someone invited by the group. Notices may be placed in the house bulletin or included on a list with other staff education seminars to be circulated round the library. Consider using slides or a video recording.

- An outline of the content of the seminar should be included with the notice when possible. The content may vary somewhat from year to year. A written summary or briefing might also be issued following the meeting, or perhaps as a substitute for the meeting or for those unable to attend.

Insurance

The insurance needs of libraries vary according to the size of the library, the design and construction of the building, the level of protection the library enjoys against various perils, and the nature of its collections.

Checking the terms of your policy

Check the terms of any insurance policy covering the library, its buildings and its holdings, noting the following points:

- Types of damage covered: fire, smoke damage, theft, storm damage, explosion, riot, water damage from defective plumbing, floods, earthquake, etc.

- Whether cover is for the full cost of replacement, or whether a deduction will be made for depreciation.

- The maximum value of the policy and whether there is a cash limit in respect of any individual item to be replaced or repaired.

- Whether the policy specifies any amount that will be payable by the insured in any loss before any contribution is paid by the insurance carrier (i.e. an "excess" or "deductible"), and how much that is. Where a library is part of a large university or government entity, it would not be unusual for it to be "self-insured" in this way.

- Whether there is special provision for individual items of great value and, if there is, whether such items are insured for their full value.

23

Incident reports

Report any accident, or other incident that may result in a claim being made, as soon as possible so that the insurance provider can undertake an immediate investigation. Bear in mind that full settlement of a claim may need to wait until the lost and damaged materials have been listed and their values have been established. Where library materials have been damaged by water, it may be better to stabilize the condition of materials by freezing them than to allow them to be discarded in the midst of the crisis (however badly damaged). Proper inspection of damaged materials and the planned salvage of valuable materials is the best way to ensure that the degree of loss can be quickly and accurately assessed and sound judgements made regarding compensation.

Suggestions:

- If the incident has been reported by telephone in the first instance, write a letter to confirm what was said.

- Ensure that an incident report is drawn up following any event that occurs on the library premises or that relates to the library that might lead to a claim being made against the library.

4. Salvaging water-damaged library materials

Aims: To salvage the holdings in such a way as to minimize the cost of recovery (including replacement and future restoration), and to rescue the maximum quantity of material from priority areas.

In the event of fire, the building will be evacuated and re-entry to the building will depend on obtaining the permission of the Fire Officer in charge. After a major fire, the building may stay hot for a long time, and re-entry may be delayed for a week or more. Some parts of the building may have collapsed or be in an unsafe condition. Other parts of the building may be structurally sound, but may have been hosed down by the fire fighters, and the warm and damp conditions will lead to rapid mould growth. The need to salvage the Library's stock should be explained to the Fire Officer in charge.

The fire service may also offer to pump out flooded premises, but if this is required in a situation where no fire has occurred, it will be regarded as a special service and the cost may have to be charged to the library. The following guidelines are typical of those to be found in library handbooks, or which have emerged from reports of disasters, and have been drawn up to provide a planned approach both to large and small incidents.

Getting started

The first step may need to be the removal of standing water so as to allow access to damaged holdings and to help reduce the general humidity in the area. Consider turning off the heat and opening windows and doors to increase ventilation. The character and degree of damage should be assessed as soon as possible.

Calling in tradesmen

Call in tradesmen as necessary, but do not allow non-urgent repair work to delay more urgent salvage work. Safety will be the primary concern. A number of problems may need to be dealt with immediately, for example:

- Electrical faults or a need for emergency lighting.

- Plumbing faults, leaking pipes, overflows, standing water.

25

- Security problems, broken windows or doors, damaged locks.

- Collapsing shelving, or damaged ceilings, which would make it dangerous to allow salvage of the holdings to proceed.

Safety checks

Enter the disaster area only when it is safe to do so. It might be wise to wait until there are more people available so that everyone who enters is accompanied by another person for safety's sake. There may be a risk of electrocution following a leak or burst pipe, due to water from firemen's hoses, or in flood situations. The risk is greater when standing water is present.

Points to consider:

- Water itself may constitute a hazard if it causes surfaces to become slippery. If floors are wet in public areas, it may be necessary to post a notice to warn staff and users of the library of the danger. It would be well to consider whether a claim for damages might be made if someone were to be injured due to failure to give adequate warning.

- Leaks or floods may lead to health risks if water has leaked into the building from soil pipes, or if water has been contaminated by chemicals.

- After a fire has been put out, there may still be danger due to smoke and fumes, and a possibility that fire will restart in certain circumstances.

Improving ventilation

Reduce high temperatures and ensure ventilation is adequate. Damp books left in warm humid conditions without ventilation will be subject to rapid mould growth. If smoke and soot damage is a major problem (often due to burning plastics), the use of the air conditioning system is not recommended as the soot will damage a sophisticated system. Open windows and use fans to expel contaminated air. No-one suffering from breathing difficulties such as emphysema or asthma should enter the affected area.

Points to consider:

- If damp library materials are left more than 48 hours in temperatures over 21° Celsius (70° Fahrenheit), it is almost certain to lead to heavy mould growth.

- Dehumidifiers can be used to reduce the humidity in an enclosed space.

- As long as books remain packed on shelves mould will be limited to the outsides. Books should not be separated and fanned out to dry until suitable drying conditions are available.

- As long as material is still submerged under water or kept wet, it should not go mouldy. The danger of mould begins when drying takes place at too slow a rate in unsuitable conditions.

Sizing up the situation

Initial action
Make an initial assessment of the resources which will be required. Immediate action may be needed to protect undamaged (or lightly damaged) material, especially where water continues to enter the building, or is working its way down from floor to floor. In the case of leaking pipes, buckets may be placed underneath drips to prevent water seeping down to lower levels, and polythene sheeting can be draped over shelving. Although this work is obviously important, it should not be allowed to delay unduly the formulation of a comprehensive plan of action. Consider calling for assistance from the following:

- Subject specialists to help determine priorities.

- Conservators to act in an advisory capacity.

- Specialist salvage contractors to provide general advice or to undertake work which is outside the capabilities of the available personnel.

How to assess the damage
Identify the various types of material involved (e.g. printed books, manuscripts, archives, newspapers, periodicals, photographs, microfilms), and whether soaked or only partially wet.

Guidelines:

- External appearance is a good indicator of damage. Mis-shapen volumes with convex spines can readily be identified as belonging to the very wet category.

- Avoid opening books when wet. When paper gets wet it becomes weak and damage can easily be done.

Identifying options for salvage

Make an initial assessment of the damage to the holdings and the options which will need to be investigated. Someone may need to be assigned to the task of locating the special facilities, equipment and supplies that will be needed. Blast freezing and cold storage facilities are generally available locally, but it will still be necessary to check what capacity is available as this will vary from season to season.

Points to consider:

- Freezing can be used to provide time for thought in order to make proper arrangements for drying, to analyze the relative costs of the different drying methods available, to prepare appropriate environmental conditions, to restore the buildings affected, to estimate full recovery costs, or just to defer decisions until the value of damaged materials may be better assessed. Freezing prevents mould growth, but does not actually kill mould spores.

- If cold store facilities are not available at the blast freezing plant, onward transport of frozen material will need to be arranged. A freezer truck will generally only be needed for journeys of two hours or more.

Which materials to remove first
Decide which materials to remove first. Where a great deal of damage has been done, the most natural way to start would be to clear a pathway picking up materials which have fallen off the shelves on to the floor, and working 'in from the door and up from the floor'. Once the way has been cleared, however, a different approach may be needed. This may be one of the most crucial steps in the planning process. It is often very difficult to decide whether to remove all the wettest material first or to concentrate efforts at an early stage on the partially wet or damp material, and there is always a danger of 'the urgent crowding out the important' when working under pressure.

Points to consider:

- The most important collections could be removed first: i.e. rare and valuable collections and other materials of permanent research value, including essential bibliographic records. However, other factors may be involved: the vulnerability of the different types of media and the degree of damage they have sustained.

- When books become soaked on the shelf, they may swell so much that they get jammed, and sometimes they may actually burst out of the shelves. When flooding is recent, and books are not yet fully swollen, it may help to remove one or two books from each row to avoid lateral pressure developing on the shelf. Most damage caused by swelling takes place in the first eight hours after they have been soaked.

- The removal of standing water, and the removal of the wettest materials may help to reduce the humidity level in the affected area. Unless under threat from further incursions of water, other materials may be left in place until the wetter materials have been removed. Where water penetration is from above, the books on the top shelves are likely to be wettest; where standing water has formed, the wettest materials may be on the lowest shelves. After removing the wettest materials, the partially wet or very damp materials may be tackled. However, the process of getting the environment of the disaster area under control may well take a long time, and it may still be necessary to move all materials out of the damaged area and into a safe dry area before a significant reduction in the moisture content has been achieved.

- Perhaps the wettest materials can be left for a while on the grounds that they will get no worse. Books immersed in water are in no immediate danger of becoming mouldy. However, a serious danger may exist when they begin to dry out, so steps should be taken to deal with them promptly once they are removed. Even when the mould problem has been taken into account, books printed on coated paper should not simply be left to dry, as the leaves are liable to stick together or 'block'. They may be best kept wet until they can be sent for freezing, if they are to be reclaimed. Special consideration may be given to valuable collections containing brittle or semi-brittle paper, including common papers from the 1880s onwards, which may suffer more badly than earlier less acidic papers from prolonged immersion in water. However, if materials containing brittle paper are replaceable, they may be left until last.

What to freeze
Decide which materials should be frozen. Freezing, and storing at low temperatures, is often recommended as the safest way of stabilizing the condition of large quantities of water-damaged library materials and of preventing mould growth. A storage temperature of -29° Celsius (-20° Fahrenheit) or lower is recommended.

Points to consider:

- Though freezing may result in some damage to photographic materials, where the formation of ice crystals disrupts the emulsion layer and leaves marks on the film, if drying cannot be arranged in the time available, the materials may have to be frozen anyway.

- It is difficult to decide between air drying and freezing in some situations. It may be best to decide on freezing when in doubt, so as to leave your options open. Frozen material may later be returned to the Library and air-dried, or it may be sent on to be freeze-dried or vacuum-dried, if required.

- Experience suggests that although saturated volumes may expand even further on freezing, the additional expansion does not appear to cause any further significant damage to already distorted volumes. Research at the Library of Congress has shown that while some damage to photographic materials has been reported after freezing, no evidence of any damage to cellulosic or proteinaceous materials (e.g. paper, cloth, leather, or vellum) could be found due to freezing. Initial treatment in a blast freezer is recommended because freezing takes place more rapidly than in a cold store, and rapid freezing results in the formation of smaller ice crystals which may result in less damage to the more vulnerable media.

What to do with non-book material
Some success has been reported in the treatment of magnetic media (audio, video and computer data) by freezing and vacuum drying. Air drying of small quantities of tape would also be possible. Decide whether any photographic materials need to be sent out for specialist treatment. Some film processing specialists will undertake to clean and dry microfilm and fiche materials, as an emergency service, but they should be given as much warning as possible. The timing may be critical, so note the following guidelines:

- Badly soaked black and white photographic materials may be kept immersed in clean water for up to three days to await specialist treatment. Prior to immersion they may be placed in unsealed polythene bags for ease of handling. After three days the emulsion layer may begin to separate from the film backing.

- Unless colour materials are taken to a professional photographic service with 48 hours after immersion in water, coloured layers will separate, and dyes will become weak or may be lost altogether.

What to air-dry
Decide which materials could be air-dried or interleaved on site. Can damaged materials be taken to another building for processing?

Points to consider:

- No attempt should be made to air-dry materials until reasonable drying conditions have been established.

- Books printed on coated paper may cause special problems when they dry out as the leaves tend to stick together. Where coated paper has already begun to dry and the leaves have stuck together, the volume may be impossible to restore.

- Small numbers of books on coated paper may be successfully salvaged by interleaving. If there are too many to deal with in the time available, they may have to be frozen.

What to leave for the experts
Decide whether there is any work which must be done under expert supervision or which can only be done by people with specialist skills. For example, under certain circumstances it might be possible to dry books by hanging them on lines, but as wet materials are easily damaged the process is not without risk. The following processes may also need to be considered and are described in more detail in the section on procedures requiring expert supervision below.

- Cleaning off mud after a river flood. As a general rule, the safest time to clean materials is after thcy have dried. However, some materials may benefit from partial cleaning while wet.

- Separating wet sheets. Generally speaking, it is inadvisable to attempt to separate wet sheets during the salvage operation. If piles of wet papers are to be frozen, you may not need to separate them, and risk further damage. Freezing while wet is usually advised, but there may be circumstances where separation of a pile of material and air drying is worth while.

Building a salvage team

Reports of disasters mention the difficulty of the work involved in salvage, how much has to be done in a very short time, the need to look out for the welfare of members of the salvage team, and the need for adequate briefing of all those involved. The work is likely to be difficult, dirty, dull and even depressing. Experience has shown that work groups perform best when given frequent short rest periods every hour or two.

Assembling a workforce

Decide what further assistance will be needed on site, and ensure that the appropriate equipment and materials will be available when needed.

Points to consider:

- Opportunities for training will be limited. Team members should be calm, adaptable, able-bodied, able to get on well with colleagues, and willing to work to strict guidelines.

- Boxes or crates may be used when material is to be moved large distances. 'Human chains' may be needed in some situations. Some heavy physical work may be needed.

- When organising work groups, care should be taken to deploy staff rationally so as to avoid bottlenecks in the removal, drying, or packing of material.

Duties and expectations
Establish duties and responsibilities before assembling a large work force of staff or volunteers. Take care how the term "volunteers" is used in relation to staff as it may be taken to suggest that employees are expected to contribute extra hours to the salvage of the holdings without compensation. Although the library may have benefitted from the generosity of staff in responding to emergencies in the past, it would be prudent to consider the possibility of conflict and disagreement over conditions.

Points to consider:

- Do not ask people to report in before you need them, but do allow enough time for them to travel to the site and to assemble.

- All team members will need rest periods, access to toilet and washing facilities, a secure place to leave belongings, and food and drink. Resting and taking refreshments in the work area may save time but could be dangerous.

Briefing the team

Handling books, maps and non-book media
Make sure the whole work force is briefed, and that everyone is aware of the dangers of handling wet, or smoke-damaged materials. No attempt should be made to restore damaged materials during the salvage operation. Further damage is likely to result when working under pressure. No attempt should be made to unwind or separate damaged microforms or deal with diskettes. Seek expert advice. Books found open and wet may be severely swollen. When a book gets wet, the paper of the text-block is liable to swell more than the covering material. The text-block generally expands in such a way that the spine assumes a concave shape, and tends to come out of the cover. No attempt should be made to close books in this state. Wet sheets of paper do not slide past each other; they tend to stick together and they tear very easily.

Guidelines:

- Avoid doing anything which might remove or deface identifying marks and labels.

- When books become soaked on the shelf, they may swell so much that they get jammed. When books are jammed, extra care may be needed, as damage may result when trying to pull them from the shelves.

- Wet materials should not be piled on top of each other in such a way as to cause heavy pressure or crushing as this may lead to increased restoration costs. Avoid applying undue pressure to distorted books or causing leaves to stick together.

- If large maps, plans, etc., have got wet and have to be moved flat, they may need to be interleaved with paper and/or polythene sheeting, and be supported with sheets of hardboard, plywood or millboard.

- Seek expert advice for treatment of non-print materials.

Organizing groups
Appoint group organizers and ensure the line of authority is clear. If consultation is required, ideas and suggestions should be genuinely welcomed. A number of groups may be needed in dealing with a large incident, or when a complex series of operations has to be set up, possibly in different parts of the building or in different buildings. It would be best to keep work groups fairly small while ensuring each group includes people with a knowledge of the collections and who are familiar with the guidelines. It may need to be made clear who will cover in the absence of the organizer.

Points to consider:

- Organizers may need to give their own groups an initial briefing, to follow this up with progress reports, and to keep their groups aware of new developments.

- Organizers should ensure that grievances are dealt with promptly, and take appropriate action on matters likely to disrupt the group. They should set standards of behaviour by example, and be prepared to represent the feelings of the group when required.

Record keeping
Ensure work groups are briefed on the need for orderly procedures in removing stock from the shelving, and the need for record keeping. If written records are to be kept, show a sample of the form to be used and explain the type of information which would be useful. Demonstrate the use of any recording

equipment to be provided. In the case of a major disaster, it may be necessary to talk about security, as there could be numbers of people coming and going all the time and there could be a lot of unfamiliar faces among them. One person in each area could be given responsibility for making an inventory, and for checking people in and out.

Guidelines:

- While it is often essential to sort materials into categories depending on degree of damage, empty shelving systematically where possible, so as to facilitate recording on damage lists, and to minimize the need for sorting when materials are eventually returned to the shelves.

- Single sheets may create particular difficulty if they have been scattered. A note of the location in which they were found may be needed.

- When recording damage, note the different types of material encountered, e.g. whether the paper is known to be highly acidic, whether it is in manuscript or printed, or some sort of photographic material (when filling out damage lists, try to use separate sheets for the different categories of material). Note the type of damage found, e.g. whether the item is soaked or only partially wet, whether the leaves are blocked (stuck together), or whether mould is found.

- A record should be made of all items to be sent outside the library for freezing, or any other sort of treatment. Such a list may be used in evaluating the loss sustained in the disaster and in investigating the possibility of further treatment, disposal, or replacement, at a later date.

Removing stock to safety

Although it is very important to know what has been damaged (and what has not), and what has left the library, record-keeping must not be allowed to delay urgent salvage activities unduly. Detailed records may be needed later however, when it comes to drawing up an insurance claim and deciding what will need to be replaced. It may be useful to take photographs of work in progress for purposes of record. It may not be necessary for all these pictures to be of professional quality.

Establish appropriate sites where packing and air-drying activities can proceed safely. The best site for air-drying may be some distance from flood or fire damaged areas, perhaps in another building, so provision of equipment to assist in the transport of materials may also need to be considered. Ensure work groups are briefed on their particular tasks and distribute handouts if available. These should establish basic ground rules, even if requiring later amendment.

Sending books, maps and non-book media for treatment off-site

Set up a suitable area to pack damaged materials for dispatch, and analyze the different activities that are required to get the job done, e.g. passing books from shelves to work tables, making an inventory, wrapping books and packing into crates, removal of full crates, supply of empty crates and materials. Allocate tasks so as to avoid bottlenecks and achieve a good work flow.

Guidelines:

- Convenient work surfaces should be provided. Surfaces may be covered with polythene sheeting both to protect the work surface and to keep damaged materials clean.

- Most books and files may be placed in polythene bags, wrapped in polythene, or separated by sheets of polythene or freezer wrap, and then packed in crates standing upright. They should normally be packed closely enough to support one another, working carefully to avoid crushing wet materials and to prevent distortion on drying. Do not pack books too tightly; leave a little space (say, the width of a finger) between books to allow for expansion during freezing. It is recommended that books be packed with their spines downward.

- Large volumes will need to be packed flat. If large maps, charts or plans are to be sent for freezing, they may need to be packed flat between boards and polythene sheeting. Large wet sheets will be very difficult to handle. Rolled items may need to be wrapped in polythene and transported as they are. Badly distorted or crumpled materials may need to be wrapped in polythene and sent for freezing as found.

- Water-damaged microforms, photographic prints and negatives could be immersed in buckets of clean water for transport to a processing laboratory. The buckets should have close-fitting lids. It is recommended that black and white material should not be left wet for more than three days, and colour material for no more than two days. Other non-book media could be packed in polythene bags to be sent for freezing as found.

- It may be best to freeze papers enclosed in boxes or folders just as they are.

- Mouldy materials, and any very acidic materials, should be packed separately and marked as such, if possible.

- Books with vellum bindings may be wrapped round with crepe bandage to prevent distortion, the bandage being secured with a safety pin.

- Do not overfill crates due to the danger of crushing the contents when the crates are stacked. Crates would normally be stacked on to wooden pallets before being loaded into a blast freezer. Take extra care if stacking cardboard boxes filled with wet books, because of the danger of crushing the contents and collapse due to the weakness of the boxes.

Air-drying and interleaving water-damaged materials

Set up a suitable work area to use for air drying purposes, and analyze the different activities that are needed to get the job done, e.g. transporting wet books from water-damaged areas, fanning out books to dry, checking rate of drying, repositioning books as necessary, and checking environmental conditions. On no account should damp books be left standing around without being checked due to the danger of mould. Newly-dried books should not be packed in boxes and left without attention for more than a few days.

Guidelines:

- Heating may need to be turned off in flood-damaged areas. Although heat is a good means of drying, it increases the risk of mould growth on damp library materials. Doors and windows may need to be opened, and fans may be used so as to expel moist air from the building. De-humidifiers may be employed in enclosed areas, but may need to be emptied periodically.

- As a rule of thumb, mould growth may begin after only 48 hours in warm humid conditions, i.e. in warm weather or in unventilated conditions. Weather and ventilation, therefore, are critical factors in deciding how much time you have to air-dry safely.

- Where a drying area with a low relative humidity and good air circulation is available, books with only wet edges may be air-dried successfully, though the whole process may take up to two weeks, and progress should be monitored. Books which have been soaked are liable to distort badly when air-dried and may go mouldy before they dry. The wetter the books are the more attention they will need.

- There is no point in separating books or fanning them out until you are satisfied that the drying conditions are adequate. In the short term at least, mould is unlikely to develop except on the outer edges of books, as long as they are close together on the shelves. Books or papers packed in boxes will be similarly protected.

- Bound volumes may be stood up on their heads to dry, with the covers opened slightly. If there are not too many to deal with, the text-blocks may be supported by pieces of cardboard or other material, so as to minimize the tendency for the books to distort as they dry. Do not attempt to fan out the leaves too much: an angle of 45^0 is about maximum, if the volume is to stay upright. If books fall over, they should be stood up again or, if they cannot be made to stand up, dried in another way. Bound volumes should not be allowed to dry in a distorted shape, if it can be avoided. There is always some distortion on drying.

- Dampness will persist for some time in the inner margins, along the spine, and between boards and flyleaves. Books must be checked from time to time and repositioned.

- Books with soft covers may need to be laid flat to dry or stood up in groups, if adequate support can be arranged to keep them upright.

- A moisture barrier (such as pieces of polythene sheeting) may be placed between the cover and the text-block to protect the leaves from the slower-drying boards.

- When books are nearly dry, it may be possible to close them up, gently form them into their natural shape with a convex spine, and lay them flat. They may be held in place with a light weight, but they should not be stacked up in large piles as good air circulation will still be needed.

- Where the contents of a pamphlet box or book box are relatively dry compared with the box, they may benefit from being removed, and air-dried, or repacked in a dry box, suitably labelled.

Selecting alternative sites
Decide whether separate areas are needed to undertake the interleaving of selected materials (e.g. valuable items printed on coated paper), to dry photographic materials, or to recondition books or boxes or documents which may be only slightly damp to begin with.

Guidelines:

- Greater control over the drying process may be achieved by interleaving with clean absorbent paper. Whatman paper Grade 114 has been recommended for this purpose, cut to various convenient sizes. Newsprint (i.e. unprinted newspaper) has also been used successfully, as have certain types of printed paper. Clearly, quite a lot of paper may be needed and the procedure is time-consuming. Coloured paper, or paper printed in colour, should never be used for interleaving wet books due to the danger of staining, or of offset from the ink.

- Wet photographic prints and glass plate negatives may be rinsed in clean water and air-dried individually (in a clean, dust free area), emulsion side up. It may help if they are inclined at an angle to allow water to drain off.

- Where materials have not been directly affected by contact with water, but have stood in very humid conditions for a considerable period, they may still be in need of some air-drying. They might be reshelved with air spaces between them in a dry environment. These materials may feel dry to the touch, but may actually contain up to 30 percent water. The normal water content of paper is from 5 to 7 percent.

Procedures requiring expert supervision

The following processes have been described in the literature, but it is recommended that they should only be undertaken by experts or by volunteers working under expert supervision.

Cleaning off mud after flooding

Experience in Florence showed that the best way to remove mud was to minimize the handling of damaged books when wet and dry them thoroughly before attempting any restoration. It was found that the mud came off best when dry, but some books could benefit from partial cleaning while still wet. Waterproof clothing, waterproof boots and gloves should be available, and may be essential if a large-scale operation is envisaged.

Decide whether books will benefit from cleaning while still wet. There are many types of book which should not be washed under any circumstances. This procedure would only be appropriate in the case of books which will not be further damaged by water. This type of treatment is not suited to open books, art on paper, or photographs, or any material with water-soluble components.

Proceed as follows:

- Hold books one at a time under water, keeping the book closed, and remove surface mud using a hose with a fine spray head attached. It has been suggested that hand sprayers (sold for spraying house plants) might also work if only a few books need treatment.

- Avoid rubbing or brushing. Anything which is hard to remove should be left until after the book has been dried.

Setting up a large scale operation
Ascertain whether a larger scale of operation should be set up. This procedure might involve six or eight tanks of water, placed side by side in a line, supplied with a continuous gentle flow of fresh water entering at the bottom of each tank. Dirty water is allowed to overflow at the top of the tank. Hoses could be used but may need to be fixed in place to prevent damage to the books as they are moved in and out of the tank. Obviously the work will be very messy. An

outdoor site with good drainage should be sought, close to the disaster area. The whole area is likely to become wet and slippery, and workers may need duck-boards to stand on. Tanks must be rust-proof. Plastic bins (garbage cans) with a capacity of twenty to thirty gallons (or 75 to 100 litres) may be suitable.

Proceed as follows:

- Books should be immersed one at a time in each tank in turn. The book should be kept closed throughout the process and gently agitated under the water to remove surface mud.

- No brushing or rubbing should be attempted, but at the last tank the books may be rinsed by spraying. It is recommended that any deposit which is not removed by this procedure should be left until after drying.

- After leaving the final tank, the book may be squeezed with hand pressure to remove some of the water. The use of mechanical presses is considered too risky.

Separating single sheets while wet

As a general rule, single sheet material found stuck together in a mass should be frozen without delay. Wet sheets should not be separated for much the same reasons that wet books should not be opened. Similarly masses of wet sheets should not be pulled out or allowed to fall out of boxes or drawers. Sheets will normally separate easily when freeze or vacuum dried; the main exception being sheets of coated paper which started to dry out and stuck together before they were frozen. It may be necessary to attempt the separation of wct sheets in some cases, however.

Decide whether the circumstances justify an attempt to separate single sheets, and ascertain what facilities would be needed to undertake the separation safely. The recommended procedure requires the use of pieces of uncoated, clear 75 micron (3 mil) polyester film and non-woven polyester web of the type used in paper conservation. The materials need to be cut to convenient sizes ready for use.

Proceed as follows:

- Dampen a sheet of clear polyester and lay it on top of a pile of wet sheets. Rub the polyester down by hand or with a bone folder, as necessary. Ease away several sheets starting at one corner of the pile, and roll or peel these back using the polyester to support the weakened paper. The surface energy of water makes it possible for the polyester to hold on to the paper.

- Transfer the polyester sheet with wet paper attached to a nearby table and lay it polyester side down making a new pile. Tables may be covered with a large pieces of polythene (polyethylene sheet) to make them serviceable as wet benches.

- Lay another piece of polyester film on top on the new pile, and try to ease the film back so as to remove a single sheet. The wet paper should attach itself to the polyester in the same way as before. Careful, gentle handling is required.

- Place this also on the table polyester side down, and lay a piece of dry polyester web on the top. The polyester web will be used for interleaving the separate sheets.

- Turn the materials over on a dry area of the table so that the polyester web is now face down, and lay a second piece of dry polyester web on top. This process can be repeated, using polyester film to separate the sheets and polyester web for interleaving, until all the sheets have been separated.

Drying options
Ascertain whether it would be best to freeze the separated sheets or whether to go on to dry the materials immediately by hand. If air-drying is feasible, each sheet could be laid out on a table (still sandwiched with polyester web on each side), or supported on nylon lines, to dry naturally. Good drying conditions will be needed. Windows might be opened, and fans may be used, but strong currents of air must not be allowed to blow directly on to the sheets. A de-humidificr might also be useful. Once a reasonable work flow has been established, with sheets being separated and air-dried in batches, it should be possible to estimate the likely rate of progress.

5. Conservation

Aims: To identify material in need of further treatment, and to plan and implement a programme of work appropriate to the material selected and its anticipated use.

In view of the high costs generally involved in the restoration of badly damaged books, full conservation treatment cannot always be justified. The possibility of replacing badly damaged books with better copies should be considered. A full assessment might need to include the cost of initial salvage work, restoration, and substitution by microfilm, photocopying, etc.

Sorting damaged holdings

Though the library may be covered by insurance, full settlement of a claim for fire or flood damage may have to wait until all the lost or damaged materials have been listed and their values have been established. An inventory made during the salvage operation may prove to be of great value. Every item may need to be made available for inspection.

Loss evaluation

Ascertain how much damage the holdings have sustained. Experience shows that not all material damaged by fire or water need be abandoned or discarded. At the same time, not all damaged material need be reclaimed. Cost will be a factor. As a general rule, most water-damaged library materials can be restored to usable condition. Exceptions might include the following:

- Books printed on coated paper, if the leaves have already stuck together. If books on coated paper are frozen while still wet (i.e. with a film of water between the leaves), there is a good chance that the book can be saved. Freeze drying has been found to be successful. Alternatively, the wet book can be interleaved with sheets of clean paper to dry the volume under controlled conditions.

- Leather bindings from the eighteenth century and later, as wetting can reduce the leather to a sort of brown sludge, and water-damaged leather from this period is often reported as being impossible to restore. By

41

contrast water-damaged bindings made from skin materials of earlier centuries has been restored successfully if dried carefully under controlled conditions.

Choosing what to replace or restore
Ascertain whether damaged stock can be replaced. This may be a fairly simple matter if they are still in print. With older books and maps it may be much more difficult. As a general rule, when books are found to be badly damaged, the combined cost of their salvage and restoration would not be justified, if they could be replaced by better copies. Various types of material may be considered for replacement including:

- Materials which have been burned or badly damaged by water, and also smoke-damaged materials, which would require too much cleaning or restoration.

- Books with less obvious signs of damage, but which will not stand up to the use anticipated for them because of weakening of the binding structure or embrittlement of materials due to exposure to heat or dampness.

- General circulating works, fiction, multiple copies, and items in high demand where either the cost of treatment or the delay involved in bringing the items back into use would be unreasonable.

- Non-book media still available from suppliers.

Drying frozen materials

Obtain expert advice on drying methods. Freeze or vacuum drying is often considered the only practical treatment for some types of water-damaged library materials: books printed on coated paper, masses of paper stuck together, magnetic media, manuscripts with fugitive inks, and hand-coloured prints, maps, etc.

Points to consider:

- The cost of treatment may depend on a number of factors and may vary greatly depending upon the circumstances of the case. Reports suggest that if a very large number of books have been damaged, and large-scale facilities are available, freeze or vacuum drying may be cheaper and more successful than air drying. An objective analysis of the relative costs of different methods of drying may be useful.

- Water-sensitive inks and other media may be very much less liable to diffuse if freeze-dried, than if dried conventionally. This treatment may also reduce the tendency for stains to develop in the paper, and may reduce the odour caused by smoke.

LEEDS METROPOLITAN
UNIVERSITY
LIBRARY

- Vacuum drying is more energy-efficient than freeze drying and should therefore be cheaper. However, as materials are dried at ambient temperatures there is a risk that mould could develop during treatment. Moreover, freeze drying may be safer for water-sensitive inks and colours. The size of the facility will also have a bearing on the cost.

- When a large scale freeze or vacuum drying operation is planned, it may be useful to estimate the quantity of water to be extracted. The Library of Congress has estimated that following prolonged immersion in water, library materials produced before 1840 will be found, on average, to contain about 80 percent water. Modern books (other than the most brittle books) will be found to contain about 60 percent water.

- Highly acidic materials should not be mixed with other materials during drying, due to the possibility of acid migration. Likewise, mouldy material should be treated separately.

Treatment of materials found to be mouldy

Checking moisture content
Ensure material is well dried out. A moisture meter (such as the 'Aquaboy') can be used to measure the moisture content. Bear in mind that the normal moisture content of printed materials is 5 to 7 percent. As the paper at the spine of the book and the boards will take longer to dry out, it is generally necessary to err on the side of over-drying when dealing with quantities of books.

Guidelines:

- Books and documents to be air-dried will need to be transferred to an environment with a relative humidity (RH) of between 35 and 40 percent (preferably with a temperature of no more than 18° Celsius or 65° Fahrenheit), and should be left to dry thoroughly. This will normally render the mould inactive, though the spores still have the potential to become active under damp conditions.

- Sometimes materials which have been freeze-dried may have already been 'over-dried' while in the treatment chamber. However, it cannot be assumed that all materials returned after treatment will be perfectly dried.

Health and safety matters
Ensure health and safety factors have been considered before attempting to kill mould spores or to remove mould from library materials. Mould can cause allergic reactions, and in rare cases can cause disease.

Guidelines:

- Fumigation treatment to kill mould spores should only be undertaken by specialists working to the highest safety standards. The use of fungicides in the stacks is no longer recommended. If a large quantity of fungicide is needed, it should be contained in a sealed chamber and recovered after use or dispersed safely to the outside. It may be possible to have a chamber set up on the library's own premises to avoid the need to transport materials long distances. However, residual fungicide left in books after treatment may also pose a threat to health.

- Treatment to remove mould growth from library materials should be undertaken only by trained staff under expert supervision. It may need to be brushed out laboriously page by page. Once dried the mould can be brushed out in a fume cupboard vented to the outside, or brushed out while working outdoors. If an industrial vacuum cleaner is used to remove the mould, it will need to be fitted with a special filter (such as a high efficiency particulate air filter), or be vented to the outside.

Storage of sterilized material
Ensure sterilized material is kept in the correct environmental conditions after treatment, and is not stored next to unsterilized mouldy materials. Sterilized material can be reinfected by mould, unless there is enough residual chemical present to prevent it.

Monitoring the storage environment after treatment

Transfer damaged materials to open shelving in a dry, well ventilated area, once they have dried out thoroughly. Random checks should be made to see whether any mould develops during storage. If material has been sterilized with chemicals, it may be necessary to monitor for residual chemicals in the storage environment too.

Points to consider:

- No water-damaged material should be returned to a high humidity environment (such as that found naturally in some climates, and as often specified for air-conditioned areas for the special collections and archives) without having first been rehabilitated in a cool dry area and monitored for mould growth.

- A rehabilitation period of at least six months has been recommended. If environmental controls are available in the rehabilitation area, it is recommended that the RH may be set at 35 or 45 percent for the first six months and then increased gradually to match the desired conditions for long-term storage.

Documentation

When material is selected for examination with a view to treatment, or a survey is proposed, consideration should be given to what background information will be required to serve as a brief. It is always desirable that both the initial brief and the eventual findings be put in writing. Treatment records should also be kept.

Preparing a brief

Explain the intrinsic value of the material under consideration and the relative value of the different components and give an indication of its present and expected future use. The brief could include:

- A description of the material and its importance in the national context, bearing in mind that if more than one type of material is to be included, these should be clearly distinguished and described separately.

- A description of the conditions in which each type of material is currently housed, e.g. the type of shelving, temperature and humidity controls, and security arrangements.

- Details of any existing catalogues, indexes or lists, and any special restrictions which have been placed on the use of the material.

Condition report

Examine the condition of the materials and ask someone to prepare a condition report before any major treatment is undertaken, describing how the materials have been altered or have deteriorated, and the location of any marked instances of change with enough detail to allow another examiner to check the observations made (e.g. existing repair work, damage due to chemical deterioration, weakness or distortion due to mould or water damage, or torn material). A condition report could also include:

- A general description of the materials examined accompanied by any call numbers, or measurements taken, which would help to identify the materials unambiguously, bearing in mind the need to distinguish different types of material clearly and describe them separately.

- An indication of the physical, chemical, or biological identification of the materials found, and the way in which they have been combined in construction.

- An indication of any treatment under consideration.

Proposals for treatment

Formal proposals may need to be drawn up before treatment begins. Documentation would include an outline of the facts of the case, a copy of the Condition Report, a summary of the work required and the implications which the treatment may have for the future use or storage of the materials. Documentation would also identify who is to do the work and may give a breakdown of the costs and contain a timetable including:

- Start date.

- Date when an interim report is due.

- Completion date.

- Date when the final report is due.

Record of treatment

Ensure that a record is made of treatment processes used, indicating how any part of the item or product of deterioration was removed, and how the item was altered to correct any distortion in shape, or to reinforce or stabilize its structure or surface. A treatment record could also include:

- An account of the condition of the material before treatment, the plan of work and the date of completion.

- A description of the processes of repair chosen and where they have been employed, along with descriptions of the materials used which may be of assistance to colleagues.

- Verbal descriptions, diagrams and photographic records, to record details observed during treatment, or to illustrate methods used, and results obtained.

Contracting out

Conservation work may need to be contracted out, and when any major conservation project is proposed, competitive tenders may be required. If funding is being sought externally, the insurance provider or other body may appoint a consultant who may ask to see all documentation and be allowed to check work in progress. Establish at the outset which processes will be undertaken directly by the contractor and which will be subcontracted.

Using your own consultants

Decide whether the library needs to employ its own consultant. In the interests of objectivity, it would be necessary to ensure that the consultant is not obligated to any supplier, manufacturer or contractor. Employing a consultant should enable the library to avoid errors, achieve economies, and take advantage of the poor experience others have had on similar projects. The consultant could survey damaged holdings, and quantify the work required. Consultants can also be instructed to do the following things:

- To specify the methods, materials, and equipment to be used.

- To negotiate with potential contractors (on clients' behalf) ensuring the contractor has the capacity, equipment, and experience to do the work.

- To draw up the terms of the contract (which may follow a standard format designed to protect the interests of all concerned), to be agreed between the client and the contractor.

- To invite offers from a number of potential contractors. The client is not necessarily obliged to accept the lowest or any other tender.

6. Annotated Further Reading

There is a growing literature on the subject of disaster planning, fire prevention and security matters for libraries. Co-operative disaster planning activities are regularly reported, particularly in Conservation Administration News (or CAN).

Planning manuals

Waters, Peter. Procedures for the Salvage of Water-damaged Library Materials. Washington: Library of Congress, 1979

> The classic guide to salvage procedures drawing on experience gained in the Florence flood of 1966 and in dealing with a number of major US disasters in the 1970s. Some of the advice is now rather dated due to changing attitudes regarding the use of fungicides. Extracts of a revised text have been issued as a reprint in A Primer of Disaster Preparedness... (see below).

Waters, P., Merritt, J. and others. A Primer on Disaster Preparedness, Management, and Response: Paper-based Materials. Selected Reprints issued by Smithsonian Institution, National Archives and Records Administration, Library of Congress, and National Park Service. Washington: October 1993 (available from the Library of Congress).

> This is a collaborative publication dealing with response to severe storms, bomb threats, earthquake, etc. (Smithsonian Institution, Office of Risk Management), advice on the salvage of flood-damaged family papers (National Archives & Records Administration), revision of the original text of Peter Waters' Procedures..., and the prevention of mould and mildew (National Park Service).

Anderson, H. and McIntyre, J. Planning Manual for Disaster Control in Scottish Libraries and Record Offices. Edinburgh: National Library of Scotland, 1985.

> A well-organized manual published as a result of a project to develop a national disaster plan for Scotland. Lists a range of professional services available in the UK, particularly in Scotland.

Morris, John. Library Disaster Preparedness Handbook. Chicago and London: American Library Association, 1986

> Discusses building design and security, problem patrons, theft, fire, water damage, conservation, etc., and concludes with a section on insurance and risk management. Written by a loss control consultant.

England, C. and Evans, K. Disaster Management for Libraries: Planning and Process. Canadian Library Association, 1988.

Text-book covering a wide range of disaster planning issues, divided into three sections: anticipating disaster, reacting to disaster, and preserving collections. Discussion includes both the 'acute disaster' and the 'quiet disaster' resulting from the gradual deterioration of library materials, and contains numerous references and endnotes.

Tregarthen Jenkin, I. Disaster Planning and Preparedness: An Outline Disaster Control Plan. British Library Information Guide 5. London: British Library, 1987.

Published as a result of a two-stage project funded by the Research and Development Department of the British Library, the first stage having comprised a survey concerned with the state of disaster planning in England, Wales and Northern Ireland, and current needs. Contains lengthy extracts from the disaster plans of three university libraries, the National Library of Scotland, the British Library, and the British Museum.

Case studies and reports

Myers, J. and Bedford, D. (editors). Disasters: Prevention and Coping. Proceedings of the Conference, May 21-22, 1980. Stanford, California: Stanford University Libraries, 1981.

Contains a report of the Stanford Meyer Library flood of 1978 (parts of which were also published in College & Research Libraries, 40 (September and November 1979). Also contains general guidance and reviews of earlier disasters, contributions on fire precautions and disaster prevention, long-term preservation issues and the 'quiet disaster', and co-operation between libraries to meet disaster planning needs.

Morris, J. Los Angeles Library Fire - Learning the Hard Way. Canadian Library Journal, 1987, 44 (4), pp 217-221.

The Central Library was struck by fire in April 1986 due to arson. 375,000 books were destroyed and another 700,000 wet books were sent to be frozen. The cost of damage to the building and its holdings was estimated tentatively at US$22 million. The open design of the building is blamed for the way the fire spread and the difficulty of controlling the blaze.

Underhill, K. and Butler, R. 'Twas the Day after Christmas...' The Northern Arizona University Cline Library Flood. Conservation Administration News. July 1991, No 46, pp 12-14.

Reports on flood damage due to a burst in a two inch (50 mm) water main crossing the ceiling over library stacks. 14760 volumes were removed, 2358 were air-dried, 2369 were frozen (and later freeze-dried), 76 volumes were repaired and 2 were declared a loss. By day six 1200 hours had been expended in salvaging the stock. The total cost of recovery is not given, but the article concludes that the operation was very successful.

News Notes. Soviet Library Fire, CAN. July 1991, No 34, p 16

Report of a fire at the USSR Academy of Sciences, on the 14th and 15th February 1988, preliminary estimates suggesting that 400,000 volumes had to be declared lost, 3,600,000 further volumes had been damaged by water or humidity, and 10,000 had been damaged by mould. Citizens of Leningrad took some 800,000 volumes home to be dried, and all were returned safely.

Belyaeva, I. Phased Conservation at the Library of the USSR Academy of Sciences. CAN, July 1991, 46, pp 1,2, and 7

Describes the efforts made to establish a programme of conservation following the disastrous fire of 1988. Steps include separation of 17th and 18th century materials from the 19th and 20th century stock which is in greater demand; the replacement where possible of damaged 19th and 20th century editions; the making of made-to-measure boxes for damaged materials (and cleaning of those materials), and encapsulation of single sheet material, to be followed by restoration of individual books in due course.

Donnelly, H. Disaster Planning in the 90's: Getting It Right. CAN. No 52 January 1993, pp 10 and 11.Donnelly, H. Disaster Planning: A Wider Approach. CAN. No 53 April 1993, pp 8, 9 and 33.

It is pointed out that many company disaster plans are concerned mostly with loss of computer data and the articles emphasize the wider aspects of the subject including health and safety, and stress. A disaster plan can never be fully comprehensive. The author is the founder of Data & Archival Damage Control Centre in the UK, and Donnelly Damage Control in the US.

Holland, M. and Landis, L. Records Recovery and Terrorism. CAN. October 1991, No 47, pp 1, 2, 3, 15 and 22.

Discusses experience at Oregon State University following an attack by animal rights activists, in which a member of staff was injured and records were damaged in an attempt to interrupt research work.

Bridgeman, C. Foolproof Solutions for the Foolhardy. Disaster Recovery Journal, April-June 1994, Vol. 7 (2), p.77.

Discusses the many ways in which computer data can be lost, even without a fire or natural disaster to complicate matters. Author is employed at Data Retrieval Services, Inc., Clearwater, Florida.

Stagnitto, J. The Shrink Wrap Project at Rutgers University Special Collections and Archives, in American Institute for Conservation Book and Paper Group Annual, and reprinted in Abbey Newsletter, Aug-Sept 1994, vol. 18 (4-5), pp 56 to 59.

Discusses a project organized and completed within a three-week period to shrink-wrap some 30,000 items to protect the collections in situ during major construction work. Total cost of the project is reported at just over US$7,000. A quite remarkable achievement.

Schnare, R. and Curtis, M. Fire Aftermath and the Recovery Process. CAN, October 1988, No 35, PP 1,2 and 22.

Schnare, R. Incendiary Gilt: When Your Labels go Up In Smoke. CAN, January 1989, No 36, pp 1-2.

Articles report experience following a fire in which smoke-damage not water-damage was the major problem. A contract was awarded to Blackmon-Mooring-Steamatic Catastrophe, Inc., to clean some 28,000 volumes of reference materials and periodicals The work was done on the library premises, and was completed within two weeks. However 1800 volumes lost the gilt lettering on the spines and a second project had to be organized to get new spine strips for the damaged volumes.

Butler, R. Disaster Planning in Nevada, CAN, January 1992, No. 48, pp 4-5.

Article reports on the success of two meetings held in Nevada: one in Reno which drew 20 people from the northern half of the state, and one in Las Vegas which drew 27 people from the southern half. Meetings covered a wide range of topics from prevention to recovery procedures and included a simulated small-scale disaster providing all participants with some 'hands-on' experience with wet books. One of the primary goals of the meetings was to 'explain the value of networking and encourage its implementation in Nevada'. An immediate interest was shown in establishing networks to assist in writing plans, training staff and providing emergency aid on a reciprocal basis. Similar regional or state-wide events have been organized in a number of other parts the US.

Fire protection and security

Fennelly, Laurence J. (editor). Museum, Archive and Library Security, Boston and London: Butterworths, 1983.

A comprehensive textbook with contributions from twenty-two experts in the field.

Turner, A. It Comes with the Territory. Handling Problem Situations in Libraries. Jefferson, North Carolina, and London: McFarland & Company, 1993.

Concerned with how to deal with poor behaviour from patrons, setting standards, and security matters. The chapter on writing good manuals begins with the proposition that there are only two kinds of library staff manual, the kind people read or use, and the kind they don't.

Morris, J. Managing the Library Fire Risk. Berkeley, California: University of California, 1979.

Discusses causes of library fires, methods of detecting and suppressing fires, and the salvage of wet books, and illustrates the point with facts concerning actual disasters and pictures of the damage sustained.

Quinsee, A. and McDonald, A. (editors). Security in Academic and Research Libraries. Proceedings of three seminars organised by SCONUL and the National Preservation Office, Newcastle-upon-Tyne: Newcastle University Library, 1991.

Discusses building design, personal safety, theft detection systems, staff awareness, attitudes and legal implications; and includes guidelines on security from the National Preservation Office (British Library).

See also the appropriate sections in Morris, Library Disaster Preparedness Handbook.